101 Easy Peasy COOKIE Recipes

ISBN-10: 1434821749

ISBN-13: 9781434821744

Contents

Bar Cookies

Drop Cookies

Drop Cookies (Cont.)

No-Bake Cookies

Rolled Cookies

Shaped Cookies

Bar Cookies

Blueberry Crumble Bars

Makes 16 bars.

    1 ½ cups quick-cooking oats

    ½ cup all-purpose flour

    ½ cup packed brown sugar

    ¼ teaspoon baking soda

    ⅛ teaspoon salt

    6 tablespoons unsalted butter or margarine, melted

    1 ½ cups fresh blueberries, rinsed and drained

    3 tablespoons granulated sugar

    2 teaspoons cornstarch

    1 teaspoon fresh lemon juice

Preheat oven to 350°F. Line an 8x8x2-inch baking pan with aluminum foil allowing ends to extend over two sides of the pan. In a large bowl, stir together oats, flour, brown sugar, baking soda, and salt. Add melted butter and stir, using a fork, until mixture becomes crumbly. Reserve ½ cup of the crumb mixture. Firmly press remaining crumb mixture into bottom of prepared baking pan. Bake for 12 minutes. Meanwhile, in a small saucepan, over medium heat, cook berries, granulated sugar, cornstarch, and lemon juice, stirring occasionally, for about two minutes or until juices are no longer cloudy. Spoon blueberry mixture over bottom layer, then sprinkle with reserved crumb mixture. Return to oven and continue baking for an additional 30 minutes. Transfer pan to a wire rack and allow cookies to cool completely before using the excess aluminum foil to lift the contents from the pan. Remove foil and cut into squares.

Butter Pecan Blondies

Makes 36 bars.

½ cup butter or margarine

2 cups firmly packed brown sugar

2 eggs

1 tablespoon vanilla extract

2 cups all-purpose flour

½ teaspoon salt

¾ cup chopped pecans

Powdered sugar

Preheat oven to 350°F. In a small saucepan, melt butter over medium heat. Stir in brown sugar. Remove from heat and allow to cool for 10 minutes. Stir in eggs and vanilla extract. Add flour and salt. Stir until well mixed. Stir in pecans. Spread into an ungreased 13x9x2-inch baking pan. Bake for 22 to 27 minutes or until set. Transfer pan to a wire rack and allow cookies to cool completely. Sprinkle with powdered sugar. Cut into bars.

Butterscotchy Pineapple Bars

Makes 24 bars.

2 ½ cups all-purpose flour

2 teaspoons baking powder

½ teaspoon salt

½ cup butter or margarine, softened

1 cup packed brown sugar

½ cup granulated sugar

3 eggs

1 teaspoon vanilla extract

1 can (20 ounces) crushed pineapple, well drained

1 cup butterscotch chips

½ cup chopped walnuts

Powdered sugar

Preheat oven to 350°F. Grease a 13x9x2-inch baking pan. In a small bowl, combine flour, baking powder, and salt. In a large bowl, with an electric mixer at medium speed, beat together butter, brown sugar, and granulated sugar until creamy. Add eggs and vanilla extract. Continue beating until well blended. Fold in crushed pineapple. Stir in flour mixture, butterscotch chips, and walnuts. Spread into prepared baking pan. Bake for 40 to 45 minutes or until a toothpick inserted in center comes out clean. Transfer pan to a wire rack and allow cookies to cool completely. Sprinkle with powdered sugar. Cut into bars.

Buttery Pineapple Crumbles

Makes 36 bars.

1 ½ cups all-purpose flour

¾ cup butter, softened, no substitutions

½ cup granulated sugar

Filling:

½ cup granulated sugar

¼ cup cornstarch

1 can (20 ounces) crushed pineapple, well drained

2 teaspoons lemon juice

⅓ cup sliced almonds

Preheat oven to 350°F. Grease a 13x9x2-inch baking pan. In a medium bowl, combine flour, butter, and ½ cup granulated sugar. With an electric mixer at low speed, beat, scraping bowl often, until mixture resembles coarse crumbs. Reserve 1 cup of flour mixture. Set aside. Press remaining crumb mixture into bottom of prepared baking pan. Bake for 10 minutes. Meanwhile, in a small saucepan, combine ½ cup granulated sugar and cornstarch. Stir in pineapple and lemon juice. Cook over medium heat, stirring constantly, for 4 to 5 minutes or until thickened. Spread filling over hot, partially baked crust. Sprinkle with reserved flour mixture. Sprinkle almonds over top. Return to oven and continue baking for 15 to 20 minutes or until lightly browned. Transfer pan to a wire rack and allow cookies to cool completely before cutting into bars.

Caramel Apple Crisps

Makes 36 bars.

1 cup packed brown sugar

½ cup butter or margarine, softened

¼ cup shortening

1 ¾ cups plus 3 tablespoons all-purpose flour, divided

1 ½ cups quick-cooking oats

1 teaspoon salt

½ teaspoon baking soda

4 ½ cups coarsely chopped, peeled, tart apples, (about 3 medium)

1 package (14 ounces) caramels, unwrapped

Preheat oven to 400°F. In a large bowl, cream together brown sugar, butter, and shortening. Stir in 1 ¾ cups flour, oats, salt, and baking soda. Reserve 2 cups of the oat mixture. Press the remaining oat mixture into an ungreased 13x9x2-inch baking pan. Stir together apples and remaining flour. Spread apple mixture over the bottom layer. In a large saucepan, heat caramels over low heat, stirring occasionally, until completely melted. Evenly pour melted caramels over the apple layer. Sprinkle with the reserved oat mixture and gently press into place. Bake for 25 to 30 minutes or until topping is golden brown and apples are tender. Cut into bars while still warm. Transfer pan to a wire rack and allow cookies to cool completely. Store, covered, in the refrigerator.

Chewy Caramel Bars

Makes 16 bars.

¾ cup all-purpose flour

1 ½ cups quick-cooking oats

⅔ cup packed brown sugar

¼ teaspoon baking soda

⅔ cup butter or margarine, melted

Filling:

25 caramels, unwrapped

2 tablespoons butter or margarine

1 tablespoon milk

½ cup chopped walnuts

Preheat oven to 350°F. Line an 8x8x2-inch baking pan with aluminum foil, allowing ends to extend over two sides of the pan. In a large bowl, stir together flour, oats, brown sugar, and baking soda. Add the melted butter and stir until well blended. Reserve 1 cup of the mixture. Press the remaining mixture into bottom of prepared baking pan. Bake for 10 minutes. Meanwhile, in a small saucepan, over low heat, cook caramels, 2 tablespoons butter, and milk, stirring constantly, until melted. Spread caramel filling over baked bottom crust. Sprinkle nuts and remaining oat mixture over the caramel filling. Return to oven and bake for an additional 20 minutes or until top is golden. Transfer pan to a wire rack and allow cookies to cool completely before using the excess aluminum foil to lift the contents from the pan. Remove foil and cut into bars.

Chewy Cherry Crumble Bars

Makes 16 bars.

½ cup butter or margarine, softened

1 cup packed brown sugar

½ teaspoon almond or vanilla extract

1 cup all-purpose flour

1 teaspoon baking powder

1 cup quick-cooking oats

½ cup cherry preserves

Preheat oven to 350°F. Grease an 8x8x2-inch baking pan. In a medium bowl, cream together butter and brown sugar. Stir in extract. Add flour, baking powder, and oats. Stir until mixture becomes crumbly. Reserve ¼ cup of the mixture. Press remaining mixture into bottom of prepared pan. Drop preserves by teaspoonfuls over the bottom layer, then sprinkle with reserved crumb mixture. Bake for 30 to 40 minutes or until browned. Transfer pan to a wire rack and allow cookies to cool completely before cutting into bars.

Chocolate Caramel Bars with a Twist

Makes 36 bars.

¾ cup packed brown sugar

¾ cup butter or margarine, softened

1 egg

1 ½ cups all-purpose flour

1 cup old-fashioned or quick-cooking oats

1 bag (14 ounces) caramels, unwrapped

⅓ cup half-and-half

1 cup semi-sweet chocolate chunks

1 cup coarsely chopped mixed nuts

¼ cup broken pretzel twists

Preheat oven to 350°F. Grease a 13x9x2-inch baking pan. In a large bowl, with an electric mixer at medium speed, cream together brown sugar and butter. Beat in egg. Add flour and oats and stir until well mixed. Press into prepared pan. Bake for 15 to 20 minutes or until light golden brown. Meanwhile, in a small saucepan, cook caramels and half-and-half over low heat, stirring occasionally, until caramels are melted. Pour over crust. Sprinkle chocolate chunks, nuts, and pretzels over the caramel layer. Return to oven and bake for an additional 5 to 8 minutes or until chocolate is softened but not completely melted. Transfer pan to a wire rack and cool until chocolate is set. Cut into bars.

Chocolate Chip Brownies

Makes 36 brownies.

½ cup butter or margarine

1 package (12 ounces) semi-sweet chocolate chips, divided

3 eggs

1 ¼ cups all-purpose flour

1 cup granulated sugar

1 teaspoon vanilla extract

¼ teaspoon baking soda

½ cup chopped nuts

Preheat oven to 350°F. Grease a 13x9x2-inch baking pan. In a large saucepan, melt butter and 1 cup chocolate chips over low heat, stirring until smooth. Remove from heat and stir in eggs. Add flour, granulated sugar, vanilla extract, and baking soda. Stir until well mixed. Add nuts and remaining chocolate chips. Stir until mixed through. Spread into prepared baking pan. Bake for 18 to 22 minutes or until a toothpick inserted in the center comes out clean. Transfer pan to a wire rack and allow cookies to cool completely before cutting into bars.

Chocolate Pecan Crumble Bars

Makes 36 bars.

1 cup butter or margarine, softened

2 ¼ cups all-purpose flour

½ cup granulated sugar

¼ teaspoon salt

1 can (14 ounces) sweetened condensed milk

1 package (12 ounces) semi-sweet chocolate chips, divided

1 teaspoon vanilla extract

1 cup chopped pecans, toasted

Preheat oven to 350°F. Grease a 13x9x2-inch baking pan. In a large bowl, with an electric mixer at medium speed, beat butter for 30 seconds. With electric mixer at low speed, beat in flour, granulated sugar, and salt until crumbly. Press 2 cups of the mixture into bottom of prepared baking pan. Bake for 12 to 14 minutes or until lightly browned at edges. Meanwhile, in a small saucepan, over medium-low heat, cook sweetened condensed milk and 1 ½ cups of the chocolate chips, stirring frequently, until melted. Remove from heat and stir in vanilla extract. Pour evenly over hot crust. Stir the remaining chocolate chips and the pecans into the reserved crust mixture. Sprinkle the crust mixture over the chocolate layer. Bake for 25 to 30 minutes or until center is set. Transfer pan to a wire rack and allow cookies to cool completely before cutting into bars.

Chocolate Walnut Bars

Makes 75 bars.

1 cup butter or margarine, divided

2 cups packed brown sugar

2 eggs

4 teaspoons vanilla extract, divided

2 ½ cups all-purpose flour

1 teaspoon baking soda

3 cups quick-cooking oats

1 can (14 ounces) sweetened condensed milk

1 package (12 ounces) semi-sweet chocolate chips

1 cup chopped walnuts

Preheat oven to 350°F. Set aside 2 tablespoons of the butter. In a large bowl, with an electric mixer at medium speed, cream together brown sugar and the remaining butter. Add eggs and 2 teaspoons of vanilla extract. Beat until well mixed. In an additional large bowl, combine flour, baking soda, and oats. Gradually add oat mixture to brown sugar mixture, stirring after each addition. Set aside. In a medium saucepan, cook the reserved butter, sweetened condensed milk, and chocolate chips, over low heat, stirring occasionally, until chocolate is melted. Remove from heat and stir in walnuts and the 2 remaining teaspoons of vanilla extract. Press two-thirds (approximately 3 ⅓ cups) of the oat mixture into an ungreased 15x10x1-inch jelly-roll pan. Spread with the melted chocolate mixture. Drop small dollops of the remaining oat mixture onto the chocolate. Bake for 25 minutes or until the oat topping is lightly browned (the chocolate layer will still be moist). Transfer pan to a wire rack and allow cookies to cool completely before cutting into bars.

Chocolatey Banana Swirls

Makes 36 bars.

> 1 cup granulated sugar
>
> ½ cup butter or margarine, softened
>
> 1 ½ cups mashed ripe banana
>
> 1 egg
>
> 1 teaspoon vanilla extract
>
> 1 ½ cups all-purpose flour
>
> 1 teaspoon baking powder
>
> 1 teaspoon baking soda
>
> ½ teaspoon salt
>
> ¼ cup unsweetened cocoa
>
> Powdered sugar

Preheat oven to 350°F. Grease a 13x9x2-inch baking pan. In a large bowl, combine granulated sugar and butter. With an electric mixer at medium speed, beat, scraping bowl often, until creamy. Beat in banana, egg, and vanilla extract, scraping bowl often, until well mixed. Add flour, baking powder, baking soda, and salt. With an electric mixer at low speed, beat until well mixed. Drop 1 ½ cups of the batter by large spoonfuls into prepared baking pan. Add cocoa to the remaining batter and beat at low speed until well mixed. Drop large spoonfuls of the chocolate batter on top of the banana batter. With a knife, gently swirl the chocolate batter through the banana batter. Bake for 20 to 25 minutes or until a toothpick inserted in the center comes out clean. Transfer pan to a wire rack to cool completely. Sprinkle with powdered sugar. Cut into bars.

Chocolatey Nutty Caramel Bars

Makes 54 bars.

1 package (14 ounces) caramels, unwrapped

⅓ cup milk

2 cups all-purpose flour

2 cups quick-cooking or old-fashioned oats

1 ½ cups packed brown sugar

1 teaspoon baking soda

½ teaspoon salt

1 egg

1 cup butter or margarine, softened

1 cup semi-sweet chocolate chips

1 cup chopped walnuts

Preheat oven to 350°F. Grease a 13x9x2-inch baking pan. In a small saucepan, over low heat, cook caramels and milk, stirring frequently, until mixture is smooth and caramels are melted. In a large bowl, combine flour, oats, brown sugar, baking soda, salt, and egg. Add butter and, using a fork, stir until mixture becomes crumbly in texture. Equally divide crumble mixture and press one half into the bottom of prepared baking pan. Bake for 10 minutes. Remove from oven and sprinkle with chocolate chips and walnuts. Drizzle with caramel mixture. Sprinkle remaining crumble mixture over top. Return to oven and bake for an additional 20 to 25 minutes or until golden brown. After cooling for 30 minutes, loosen edges from sides of pan. Transfer pan to a wire rack and allow cookies to cool completely before cutting into bars.

Chocolatey Raspberry Streusel Bars

Makes 24 bars.

1 ¼ cups butter or margarine, softened, divided

1 ¼ cups granulated sugar, divided

1 egg

3 cups all-purpose flour, divided

1 package (12 ounces) semi-sweet chocolate chips, divided

1 jar (10 ounces) raspberry jam

Glaze:

1 cup powdered sugar

1 tablespoon milk

1 teaspoon vanilla extract

Preheat oven to 350°F. Grease a 13x9x2-inch baking pan. In a large bowl, with an electric mixer at medium speed, cream together 1 cup butter and 1 cup granulated sugar. Beat in egg. Beat in 2 cups of the flour. Stir in 1 cup of the chocolate chips. Spread mixture into bottom of prepared baking pan. Spread jam evenly over bottom layer to within ½-inch of the edges. In a medium bowl, stir together 1 cup flour and ¼ cup granulated sugar. Using a pastry blender, cut in ¼ cup butter until mixture is crumbly. Stir in remaining chocolate chips. Evenly sprinkle the crumble mixture over the jam layer. Bake for 40 to 45 minutes or until top is golden brown. Transfer pan to a wire rack and allow cookies to cool completely before cutting into bars. Meanwhile, in a small bowl, stir together powdered sugar, milk, and vanilla extract. Drizzle glaze over bars. Allow glaze to set before storing.

Decadent Cheesecake Bars

Makes 16 bars.

5 tablespoons butter or margarine, softened

⅓ cup packed brown sugar

1 cup all-purpose flour

½ cup granulated sugar

1 package (8 ounces) cream cheese, softened

1 egg

2 tablespoons milk

1 tablespoon lemon juice

½ teaspoon vanilla extract

Preheat oven to 350°F. Lightly coat an 8x8x2-inch baking pan with cooking spray. In a medium bowl, use a fork to stir together butter, brown sugar, and flour until mixture resembles coarse crumbs. Reserve 1 cup of the crumb mixture. Press mixture into bottom of prepared baking pan. Bake for 15 minutes. Meanwhile, in a medium bowl, cream together granulated sugar and cream cheese. Beat in egg, milk, lemon juice, and vanilla extract. Spread cream cheese mixture over the bottom layer. Sprinkle with the remaining crumb mixture. Return to oven and continue baking for an additional 25 minutes. Transfer pan to a wire rack to cool completely. Refrigerate for at least 1 hour before cutting into squares.

Doubly Delicious Holiday Bars

Makes 48 bars.

1 cup granulated sugar

¾ cup butter or margarine, softened

1 teaspoon vanilla extract

1 egg

2 cups all-purpose flour

1 cup diced mixed candied fruit

½ cup semi-sweet chocolate chips

½ cup chopped pecans

Glaze:

1 cup powdered sugar

1 tablespoon milk

Preheat oven to 350°F. In a large bowl, cream together granulated sugar and butter. Blend in vanilla extract and egg. Stir in flour until well mixed. Spread dough into an ungreased 15x10x1-inch jelly-roll pan. Sprinkle mixed candied fruit over half of the dough and sprinkle chocolate chips and pecans over the other half. Gently press into dough. Bake for 25 to 30 minutes or until lightly browned at edges. Transfer pan to a wire rack and allow cookies to cool completely. Meanwhile, in a small bowl, blend powdered sugar and enough milk for desired drizzling consistency. Drizzle over cooled bars. Let drizzle set before cutting into bars.

Flaky Cinnamon Shortbread

Makes 48 bars.

> 1 ½ cups all-purpose flour
>
> ¾ cup powdered sugar
>
> ½ cup cake flour
>
> 1 cup butter or margarine, softened
>
> ½ teaspoon cinnamon

Topping:

> 1 tablespoon granulated sugar
>
> ⅛ teaspoon cinnamon

Preheat oven to 350°F. Lightly grease a 13x9x2-inch baking pan. In a large bowl, combine all-purpose flour, powdered sugar, cake flour, butter, and ½ teaspoon cinnamon. With an electric mixer at low speed, beat just until a soft dough forms. Take care not to overbeat. Press dough evenly into prepared baking pan. In a small bowl, stir together topping ingredients. Sprinkle topping evenly over shortbread. Prick holes in dough with a fork. Bake for 20 to 30 minutes or until light golden brown. Transfer pan to a wire rack. Cool slightly before cutting into bars.

Frosted Double Peanut Butter Bars

Makes 36 bars.

½ cup creamy or crunchy peanut butter

¼ cup unsalted butter, softened

1 ¼ cups granulated sugar

2 eggs, lightly beaten

1 teaspoon vanilla extract

2 cups all-purpose flour

1 teaspoon baking powder

½ teaspoon salt

1 cup chopped peanuts, plus more for garnish

Frosting:

½ cup creamy peanut butter

¼ cup unsalted butter, softened

½ cup powdered sugar

Preheat oven to 350°F. Line a 13x9x2-inch baking pan with aluminum foil allowing ends to extend over the two ends of the pan. Generously coat aluminum foil with cooking spray. In a medium bowl, with an electric mixer at medium speed, beat together ½ cup peanut butter and ¼ cup butter. Add granulated sugar and beat until well blended. Beat in eggs and vanilla extract. Stir in flour, baking powder, and salt. Stir in peanuts. Evenly press mixture into bottom of prepared baking pan. Bake for 30 minutes or until edges pull away from sides of pan. Transfer pan to a wire rack and allow cookies to cool completely before using the excess aluminum foil to lift the contents from the pan. Meanwhile, in a medium bowl, with an electric mixer at medium speed, cream together ½ cup peanut butter, ¼ cup butter, and powdered sugar until smooth and fluffy. After removing the aluminum foil, spread cookies with frosting. Sprinkle with chopped peanuts, if desired. Cut into bars.

Hawaiian Bar Cookies

Makes 30 bars.

½ cup butter or margarine, softened

1 cup granulated sugar

3 eggs, beaten

1 ripe banana, mashed

2 ½ cups all-purpose flour

1 teaspoon baking soda

1 can (8 ounces) crushed pineapple

¼ teaspoon salt

¼ cup powdered sugar

¼ cup flaked coconut

Preheat oven to 350°F. Grease a 13x9x2-inch baking pan. In a large bowl, cream together butter and granulated sugar. Add eggs, banana, flour, baking soda, crushed pineapple, and salt. Stir just until mixed. Pour into prepared baking pan. Bake for 25 to 30 minutes or until a toothpick inserted in the center comes out clean. Cool for 10 minutes before sprinkling with powdered sugar and coconut. Transfer pan to a wire rack and allow cookies to cool completely before cutting into bars.

Iced Banana Bars

Makes 24 bars.

    1 cup granulated sugar

    1 cup mashed very ripe banana

    ⅓ cup vegetable oil

    2 eggs

    1 cup all-purpose flour

    1 teaspoon baking powder

    ½ teaspoon baking soda

    ½ teaspoon cinnamon

    ¼ teaspoon salt

Frosting:

    1 package (3 ounces) cream cheese, softened

    ⅓ cup butter or margarine, softened

    1 teaspoon vanilla extract

    2 cups powdered sugar

Preheat oven to 350°F. Grease a 13x9x2-inch baking pan. In a large bowl, stir together granulated sugar, banana, oil, and eggs. Mix in flour, baking powder, baking soda, cinnamon, and salt. Spread into prepared baking pan. Bake for 25 to 30 minutes or until a toothpick inserted in the center comes out clean. Transfer pan to a wire rack and allow cookies to cool completely before frosting. Meanwhile, in a medium bowl, with an electric mixer at medium speed, blend together cream cheese, butter, and vanilla extract. Using a spoon, gradually stir in powdered sugar. Continue to stir frosting until it becomes smooth and spreadable. Spread cookies with frosting, then cut into bars. Store, covered, in the refrigerator.

Key West Cookies

Makes 36 bars.

1 ½ cups coconut cookie crumbs, about 17 cookies

3 tablespoons butter or margarine, melted

1 package (8 ounces) cream cheese, softened

1 can (14 ounces) sweetened condensed milk

¼ cup Key lime juice or regular lime juice

1 tablespoon grated lime peel

Preheat oven to 350°F. Grease a 9x9x2-inch baking pan. Using a fork, combine cookie crumbs and butter. Press into bottom of prepared baking pan. Place pan in refrigerator. Meanwhile, in a small bowl, with an electric mixer at medium speed, beat cream cheese until light and fluffy. Gradually beat in sweetened condensed milk until mixture is smooth. Beat in lime juice and lime peel. Remove pan from refrigerator and evenly spread cream cheese mixture over cookie crumb layer. Bake for 35 minutes or until center is set. Transfer pan to a wire rack and allow cookies to cool for 30 minutes before cutting into bars. Refrigerate for at least 3 hours before serving. Store, covered, in refrigerator.

Malted Milk Chocolate Brownies

Makes 48 brownies.

> 1 package (11.5 ounces) milk chocolate chips
>
> ½ cup butter or margarine
>
> ¾ cup granulated sugar
>
> 1 teaspoon vanilla extract
>
> 3 eggs
>
> 1 ¾ cups all-purpose flour
>
> ½ cup instant malted milk powder
>
> ½ teaspoon baking powder
>
> ¼ teaspoon salt
>
> 1 cup malted milk balls, coarsely chopped

Preheat oven to 350°F. Grease bottom and sides of a 9x9x2-inch baking pan. In a medium saucepan, over low heat, cook milk chocolate chips and butter, stirring frequently, until melted. Remove from heat and allow to cool slightly. Stir in granulated sugar, vanilla extract, and eggs. Mix in flour, malted milk powder, baking powder, and salt. Spread into prepared baking pan. Sprinkle malted milk balls over top. Bake for 30 to 35 minutes or until a toothpick inserted in the center comes out clean. Transfer pan to a wire rack and allow cookies to cool completely before cutting into bars.

Mix-in-the-Pan Pecan Brownies

Makes 36 brownies.

½ cup butter or margarine

2 cups granulated sugar

1 cup all-purpose flour

1 cup chopped pecans

4 eggs

1 teaspoon vanilla extract

4 packets (1 ounce each) liquid unsweetened chocolate

1 teaspoon vanilla extract

Preheat oven to 350°F. In a 13x9x2-inch baking pan, melt butter in oven. Add remaining ingredients to pan and stir with a fork until well mixed. Smooth batter to edges of pan with a spatula. Bake for 25 to 30 minutes or until a toothpick inserted in the center comes out clean. Transfer pan to a wire rack and allow cookies to cool completely before cutting into bars.

Mocha Brownies

Makes 48 brownies.

½ cup shortening

½ cup butter or margarine

1 cup unsweetened cocoa

2 cups granulated sugar

4 teaspoons instant coffee granules

1 tablespoon hot water

4 eggs

2 teaspoons vanilla extract

1 cup all-purpose flour

½ teaspoon salt

Frosting:

½ cup butter or margarine, softened

2 cups powdered sugar

1 teaspoon vanilla extract

2-3 teaspoons instant coffee granules

1 ½ tablespoons milk

Preheat oven to 350°F. Grease a 13x9x2-inch pan. In a small saucepan, over low heat, stir together shortening and ½ cup butter until melted. Remove from heat and blend in cocoa. Stir in granulated sugar until well mixed. Dissolve 4 teaspoons instant coffee in hot water and combine with cocoa mixture. One at a time, stir in eggs. Add 2 teaspoons vanilla extract, flour, and salt, stirring just until mixed. Pour mixture into prepared baking pan.

Bake for 25 to 30 minutes. Transfer pan to a wire rack and allow cookies to cool completely before frosting. Meanwhile, cream together ½ cup butter and powdered sugar in a medium bowl. With an electric mixer at medium speed, mix in 1 teaspoon vanilla extract. In a small bowl, dissolve 2-3 teaspoons instant coffee in milk. Add dissolved coffee to powdered sugar mixture and beat on high speed until light and fluffy. Spread brownies with frosting and cut into bars.

Nutterscotch Bars

Makes 36 bars.

> 1 ½ cups all-purpose flour
>
> ¾ cup firmly packed brown sugar
>
> ½ cup butter or margarine, softened
>
> ¼ teaspoon salt

Topping:

> ¼ cup light corn syrup
>
> 1 cup butterscotch chips
>
> 2 tablespoons butter or margarine
>
> 1 tablespoon water
>
> ¼ teaspoon salt
>
> 1 ½ cups mixed nuts

Preheat oven to 350°F. Grease a 13x9x2-inch baking pan. In a large bowl, combine flour, brown sugar, ½ cup butter and ¼ teaspoon salt. With an electric mixer at low speed, beat, scraping bowl often, until mixture resembles coarse crumbs. Press crumb mixture into bottom of prepared baking pan. Bake for 10 minutes. Meanwhile, in a small saucepan, cook corn syrup, butterscotch chips, 2 tablespoons butter, water, and ¼ teaspoon salt over low heat, stirring constantly, for 5 to 7 minutes or until chips are melted and mixture is smooth. Add nuts and stir until well coated. Spread nut mixture over hot, partially baked crust. Return to oven and continue baking for 10 to 12 minutes or until golden brown. Transfer pan to a wire rack and allow cookies to cool completely before cutting into bars.

Nutty Nilla Brownies

Makes 32 brownies.

½ cup butter or margarine

1 package (12 ounces) white chips

1 ¼ cups all-purpose flour

¾ cup granulated sugar

½ cup chopped nuts

1 teaspoon vanilla extract

¼ teaspoon salt

3 eggs

Frosting:

1 ½ cups powdered sugar

2 tablespoons butter or margarine, softened

1 teaspoon vanilla extract

1 tablespoon milk

Preheat oven to 350°F. Grease and flour a 13x9x2-inch baking pan. In a large saucepan, over low heat, cook ½ cup butter and baking chips, stirring frequently, until melted. Mixture may appear to be curdled. Remove from heat and cool. Stir in flour, granulated sugar, nuts, 1 teaspoon vanilla extract, salt, and eggs. Spread mixture into bottom of prepared baking pan. Bake for 30 to 35 minutes or until a toothpick inserted in the center comes out clean. Transfer pan to a wire rack and allow cookies to cool completely before frosting. Meanwhile, in a medium bowl, stir together powdered sugar, 2 tablespoons butter, 1 teaspoon vanilla extract, and milk. Add more milk, if required. Spread with frosting, then cut into bars.

Peanutty Milk Chocolate Bars

Makes 24 bars.

¾ cup butter or margarine, softened

¾ cup chunky peanut butter

1 ½ cups granulated sugar

3 eggs

2 teaspoons vanilla extract

2 ½ cups all-purpose flour

1 teaspoon baking soda

1 teaspoon salt

1 package (11.5 ounces) milk chocolate chips

Preheat oven to 350°F. In a large bowl, with an electric mixer at medium-high speed, cream together butter, peanut butter, granulated sugar, eggs, and vanilla extract. Stir in flour, baking soda, and salt until well blended. Stir in chocolate chips. Press dough into an ungreased 15x10x1-inch jelly-roll pan. Bake for 20 to 22 minutes. Transfer pan to a wire rack and allow cookies to cool completely before cutting into bars.

Piña Colada-Topped Peanut Butter Bars

Makes 32 bars.

½ cup chunky peanut butter

½ cup butter or margarine

¾ cup granulated sugar

¾ cup packed brown sugar

2 eggs, beaten

½ teaspoon coconut extract

½ teaspoon vanilla extract

1 cup all-purpose flour

1 package (12 ounces) white chips, melted

⅓ cup piña colada-flavored yogurt

½ cup flaked coconut, toasted

Preheat oven to 350°F. Lightly grease a 13x9x2-inch baking pan. In a large saucepan, over medium heat, cook peanut butter and butter, stirring frequently, until melted and well blended. Remove from heat. Stir in granulated sugar, brown sugar, eggs, coconut extract, and vanilla extract. Stir in flour. Spread mixture into bottom of prepared baking pan. Bake for 18 to 20 minutes or until lightly browned. Transfer pan to a wire rack and allow cookies to cool completely before frosting. Meanwhile, in a medium bowl, stir together melted baking chips and yogurt. Spread the baking chip mixture over the bars. Sprinkle with toasted coconut. Allow topping to cool completely before cutting into bars. Store, covered, in the refrigerator.

Pineapple Bars with Caramel Drizzle

Makes 24 bars.

2 cups all-purpose flour

1 ½ cups quick-cooking or old-fashioned oats

1 teaspoon baking soda

½ cup butter or margarine, softened

1 cup packed brown sugar

2 eggs

2 tablespoons milk

1 teaspoon vanilla extract

1 can (20 ounces) crushed pineapple, well drained

½ cup caramel topping

Preheat oven to 350°F. Grease and flour a 13x9x2-inch baking pan. In a medium bowl, stir together flour, oats, and baking soda. In another medium bowl, with an electric mixer at medium speed, cream together butter and brown sugar. Stir in eggs, milk, and vanilla extract until well mixed. Gradually add flour, stirring after each addition. Gently fold in pineapple until just mixed. Spread into prepared baking pan. Bake for 20 to 25 minutes or until a toothpick inserted in the center comes out clean. Cool for 15 minutes before drizzling caramel sauce over top. Transfer pan to a wire rack and allow cookies to cool completely before cutting into bars.

Polka-Dot Brownies

Makes 36 brownies.

1 cup butter or margarine

2 cups granulated sugar

⅔ cup unsweetened cocoa

4 eggs, beaten

2 teaspoons vanilla extract

¾ cup all-purpose flour

½ teaspoon salt

¼ teaspoon baking soda

2 ½ cups miniature marshmallows

⅔ cup salted or unsalted peanuts

1 ⅓ cups candy-coated chocolate pieces

Preheat oven to 350°F. Grease 13x9x2-inch pan. In a medium saucepan, melt butter over low heat. Stir in granulated sugar and cocoa until blended. Remove from heat and stir in eggs and vanilla extract until mixed. In a medium bowl, combine flour, salt, and baking soda. Add to chocolate mixture and stir until well mixed. Spread into prepared baking pan. Bake for 25 minutes. Sprinkle with marshmallows and peanuts. Return to oven and continue baking for an additional 5 minutes or until the marshmallows are puffed and just beginning to brown. Sprinkle with candy-coated chocolate pieces and press candy lightly into marshmallows. Transfer pan to a wire rack and allow cookies to cool completely before cutting into bars. To prevent marshmallows from sticking use a wet knife to cut into bars.

Soft Ginger Bars

Makes 48 bars.

1 ¼ **cups granulated sugar**

1 **cup butter or margarine, softened**

1 **egg**

3 **tablespoons molasses**

3 **cups all-purpose flour**

1 **teaspoon baking soda**

2 **teaspoons cinnamon**

2 **teaspoons ginger**

3 **tablespoons colored decorator sugar**

Preheat oven to 350°F. In a large bowl, combine granulated sugar, butter, egg, and molasses. With an electric mixer at medium speed, beat until creamy. Add flour, baking soda, cinnamon, and ginger. With electric mixer at low speed, beat until well mixed. Press dough into an ungreased 15x10x1-inch jelly-roll pan. Sprinkle decorator sugar over top. Bake for 16 to 20 minutes or until edges are lightly browned. Transfer pan to a wire rack and allow cookies to cool completely before cutting into bars.

Southern Pecan Pie Bites

Makes 36 bars.

⅔ cup granulated sugar

½ cup butter or margarine, softened

1 teaspoon vanilla extract

1 ½ cups all-purpose flour

Filling:

⅔ cup packed brown sugar

½ cup dark corn syrup

1 teaspoon vanilla extract

¼ teaspoon salt

3 eggs

1 cup coarsely chopped pecans

Preheat over to 350°F. Lightly grease a 13x9x2-inch baking pan. In a large bowl, combine granulated sugar, butter, and 1 teaspoon vanilla extract. Stir in flour. Press into bottom and ½ inch up the sides of prepared baking pan. Bake for 15 to 17 minutes or until edges are light brown. Meanwhile, in a medium bowl, using a spoon, beat brown sugar, corn syrup, 1 teaspoon vanilla extract, salt, and eggs until well mixed. Stir in pecans. Pour filling over crust. Return to oven and continue baking for an additional 25 to 30 minutes or until filling is set. While still warm, loosen edges from sides of pan. Transfer pan to a wire rack and allow cookies to cool completely before cutting into bars.

Strawberry Strips

Makes about 24 bars.

 2 cups all-purpose flour

 ⅔ cup granulated sugar

 ½ teaspoon baking powder

 ¾ cup butter or margarine, softened

 1 egg

 2 teaspoons vanilla extract

 ⅓ cup strawberry jelly or jam

Preheat oven to 350°F. In a medium bowl, stir together flour, granulated sugar, and baking powder. Use a pastry blender to blend in butter, egg, and vanilla extract until a dough is formed. Place dough on a lightly floured surface and divide into four equal parts. Shape each piece into a 13-inch-long by ¾-inch-thick roll. Place rolls on ungreased baking sheets, about 4 inches apart and 3 inches from edges. Make a ¼ to ⅓-inch-deep indentation lengthwise down the center of each roll. Fill each indentation with jelly. Bake for 15 to 20 minutes. Cut diagonally into bars while still warm. Transfer to wire racks to cool.

Toffee Shortbread

Makes 48 bars.

> 1 cup butter or margarine, softened
>
> ½ cup granulated sugar
>
> 2 cups all-purpose flour
>
> ½ cup finely chopped walnuts
>
> ½ cup toffee baking bits

Glaze:

> 1 cup powdered sugar
>
> 1 ½ teaspoons vanilla extract
>
> 2-3 tablespoons milk

Preheat oven to 350°F. In a large bowl, cream together butter and granulated sugar. Add flour. With an electric mixer at low speed, beat until mixture forms a dough. Add walnuts and toffee bits. Hand stir until mixed through. Press dough into an ungreased 15x10x1-inch jelly-roll pan. Bake for 20 to 24 minutes or until golden brown. Cut into bars while still hot. Cool for 5 minutes. Meanwhile, in a small bowl, combine powdered sugar and vanilla extract. Gradually stir in milk until desired consistency for glazing. Spread evenly over warm shortbread. Transfer pan to a wire rack and allow cookies to cool completely.

All That Cookies

Makes about 6 dozen cookies.

1 ¼ cups butter-flavored shortening

1 ½ cups firmly packed brown sugar

1 cup granulated sugar

3 eggs

1 ¼ cups extra crunchy peanut butter

4 ½ cups quick-cooking oats

2 teaspoons baking soda

1 cup semi-sweet chocolate chips

1 cup butterscotch chips

1 cup chopped walnuts

Preheat oven to 350°F. In a large bowl, with an electric mixer at medium speed, cream together shortening, brown sugar, and granulated sugar. Mix in eggs. Add peanut butter and beat until well blended. In a medium bowl, combine oats and baking soda. Hand stir oat mixture into shortening mixture. Add chocolate chips, butterscotch chips, and nuts. Stir until blended. Drop by rounded teaspoonfuls, 2 inches apart, onto ungreased baking sheets. Bake for 10 to 11 minutes or until just lightly browned. Allow cookies to cool for 2 minutes on baking sheets, then transfer to wire racks to cool completely.

Banana Milk Chocolate Softies

Makes about 3 dozen cookies.

⅓ cup butter or margarine, softened

½ cup granulated sugar

1 egg

½ cup mashed ripe banana

½ teaspoon vanilla extract

1 cup all-purpose flour

1 teaspoon baking powder

¼ teaspoon salt

⅛ teaspoon baking soda

1 cup milk chocolate chips

Preheat oven to 350°F. Lightly grease baking sheets. In a small bowl, with an electric mixer at medium speed, cream together butter and granulated sugar. Beat in egg, banana, and vanilla extract until blended. In a medium bowl, combine flour, baking powder, salt, and baking soda. Gradually add dry ingredients to creamed mixture, beating after each addition. Fold in chocolate chips. Drop by tablespoonfuls onto prepared baking sheets. Bake for 9 to 11 minutes or until lightly browned at edges. Transfer to wire racks to cool.

Best-Ever Oatmeal Raisin Cookies

Makes about 3 dozen cookies.

2 cups all-purpose flour

1 teaspoon baking soda

1 teaspoon baking powder

1 teaspoon salt

1 cup unsalted butter, softened

1 cup granulated sugar

1 cup firmly packed brown sugar

2 eggs

2 teaspoons vanilla extract

3 cups old-fashioned oats

1 ½ cups raisins

Preheat oven to 350°F. Lightly grease baking sheets. In a large bowl, stir together flour, baking soda, baking powder, and salt. In another large bowl, with an electric mixer at low speed, cream together butter, granulated sugar, brown sugar, eggs, and vanilla extract. Add flour mixture and stir just until blended in. Do not over mix. Stir in oats and raisins. Drop by level ⅛-cupfuls, about 2 inches apart, onto prepared baking sheets. Bake for 11 to 13 minutes or until cookies are golden but still moist beneath the cracks on top. Allow cookies to cool for 2 minutes on baking sheets, then transfer to wire racks to cool completely.

Cherry Chocolate Drops

Makes about 4 ½ dozen cookies.

2 cups all-purpose flour

½ teaspoon baking powder

1 cup butter or margarine, softened

½ cup granulated sugar

1 ½ cups packed brown sugar

2 eggs

1 teaspoon vanilla extract

1 cup semi-sweet chocolate chips

3 cups old-fashioned oats

1 cup dried cherries

Preheat oven to 350°F. In a medium bowl, combine flour and baking powder. In a large bowl, with an electric mixer at medium-high speed, cream together butter, granulated sugar, and brown sugar. Add eggs and vanilla extract. Beat until well mixed. With mixer at medium speed, gradually add flour mixture, beating after each addition, until combined. Stir in chocolate chips, oats, and cherries. Drop by rounded tablespoonfuls onto ungreased baking sheets. Bake for 12 to 14 minutes or until edges are golden brown and centers are still soft. Transfer to wire racks to cool.

Cherry Coconut Cookies

Makes about 4 dozen cookies.

¾ cup butter or margarine, softened

1 cup packed brown sugar

1 egg

2 tablespoons milk

1 teaspoon vanilla extract

2 cups all-purpose flour

½ teaspoon salt

½ teaspoon baking soda

½ cup maraschino cherries, well drained and chopped

½ cup chopped pecans

½ cup flaked coconut

Preheat oven to 375°F. In a large bowl, with an electric mixer at medium speed, cream together butter and brown sugar. Add egg, milk, and vanilla extract. Beat until well blended. In a medium bowl, combine flour, salt, and baking soda. Gradually add dry ingredients to creamed mixture, beating after each addition. Stir in cherries, pecans, and coconut. Drop by teaspoonfuls onto ungreased baking sheets. Bake for 10 to 12 minutes or until golden brown. Transfer to wire racks to cool.

Chewy Chocolatey Oatmeal Cookies

Makes about 3 ½ dozen cookies.

> 1 ½ cups packed brown sugar
>
> 1 cup butter or margarine, softened
>
> 1 teaspoon vanilla extract
>
> 1 egg
>
> 2 cups quick-cooking oats
>
> 1 ½ cups all-purpose flour
>
> 1 teaspoon baking soda
>
> ¼ teaspoon salt
>
> 1 cup semi-sweet chocolate chips
>
> 1 cup chopped nuts, optional

Preheat oven to 350°F. In a large bowl, cream together brown sugar and butter. Add vanilla extract and egg. Stir until light and fluffy. Mix in oats, flour, baking soda, and salt. Mix in chocolate chips and nuts. Drop by rounded tablespoonfuls, about 2 inches apart, onto ungreased baking sheets. Bake for 9 to 11 minutes or until golden brown. Allow cookies to cool slightly on baking sheets, then transfer to wire racks to cool completely.

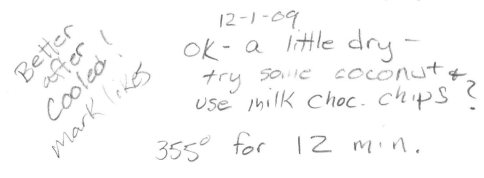

Better after cooled
Mark liked

12-1-09
OK - a little dry - try some coconut + use milk choc. chips?
355° for 12 min.

Chocolate Marshmallow Melts

Makes about 3 dozen cookies.

½ cup butter or margarine, softened

1 cup granulated sugar

1 egg

¼ cup milk

1 teaspoon vanilla extract

1 ¾ cups all-purpose flour

⅓ cup unsweetened cocoa

½ teaspoon baking soda

½ teaspoon salt

18 large marshmallows

Preheat oven to 350°F. In a large bowl, with an electric mixer at medium speed, cream together butter and granulated sugar. Beat in egg, milk, and vanilla extract. In a medium bowl, combine flour, unsweetened cocoa, baking soda, and salt. Gradually add to creamed mixture, beating after each addition. Drop by rounded teaspoonfuls onto ungreased baking sheets. Bake for 8 minutes. Meanwhile, using kitchen scissors, cut marshmallows in half. Press a marshmallow half, cut side down, onto top of each cookie. Return cookies to oven and continue baking for an additional 2 minutes. Transfer to wire racks to cool.

Choco Trio Cookies

Makes about 3 ½ dozen cookies.

1 ¾ cups all-purpose flour

½ cup unsweetened cocoa

1 teaspoon baking soda

1 package (12 ounces) semi-sweet chocolate chips, divided

⅓ cup butter or margarine, cut into pieces

1 can (14 ounces) sweetened condensed milk

1 egg

1 teaspoon vanilla extract

½ cup chopped nuts

Preheat oven to 350°F. Lightly grease baking sheets. In a medium bowl, stir together flour, cocoa, and baking soda. In a large saucepan, over low heat, melt 1 cup chocolate chips and butter. Stir until smooth. Remove from heat and add sweetened condensed milk, egg, and vanilla extract. Stir together until well mixed. Stir in flour mixture. Stir in nuts and remaining chocolate chips. (Dough will be soft in consistency.) Drop by rounded tablespoonfuls onto prepared baking sheets. Bake for 8 to 10 minutes or until edges are set but centers are still slightly soft. Allow cookies to cool for 2 minutes on baking sheets, then transfer to wire racks to cool completely.

Colossal Double Chocolate White Chip Cookies

Makes about 2 dozen cookies.

> **4 cups all-purpose flour**
>
> **1 teaspoon baking powder**
>
> **1 teaspoon baking soda**
>
> **1 ½ cups butter or margarine, softened**
>
> **1 ¼ cups granulated sugar**
>
> **1 ¼ cups packed brown sugar**
>
> **2 eggs**
>
> **1 tablespoon vanilla extract**
>
> **1 cup milk chocolate chips**
>
> **1 cup semi-sweet chocolate chips**
>
> **½ cup white chips**
>
> **1 cup chopped nuts**

Preheat oven to 350°F. In a medium bowl, stir together flour, baking powder, and baking soda. In a large bowl, cream together butter, granulated sugar, and brown sugar. Beat eggs and vanilla extract into butter mixture. Gradually stir in flour mixture. Stir in milk chocolate chips, semi-sweet chocolate chips, white chips, and nuts. Drop by level ¼-cupfuls, about 2 inches apart, onto ungreased baking sheets. Bake for 12 to 14 minutes or until light golden brown. Allow cookies to cool for 2 minutes on baking sheets, then transfer to wire racks to cool completely.

Double Chocolate Oatmeal Cookies

Makes about 2 ½ dozen cookies.

1 package (12 ounces) semi-sweet chocolate chips, divided

1 ¼ cups all-purpose flour

2 teaspoons baking powder

¼ teaspoon baking soda

¼ teaspoon salt

1 cup butter or margarine, softened

¾ cup firmly packed brown sugar

1 egg

1 teaspoon vanilla extract

2 cups quick-cooking or old-fashioned oats

Preheat oven to 350°F. In a small saucepan, over low heat, melt 1 cup of the chocolate chips. Set aside to cool. Meanwhile, in a medium bowl, stir together flour, baking powder, baking soda, and salt. In a large bowl, with an electric mixer at medium speed, cream together butter and brown sugar. Mix in melted chocolate, egg, and vanilla extract. Gradually add flour mixture, mixing after each addition. Stir in oats and remaining 1 cup chocolate chips. Drop by rounded tablespoonfuls onto ungreased baking sheets. Bake for 12 to 14 minutes or until cookies are set. Allow cookies to cool for 2 minutes on baking sheets, then transfer to wire racks to cool completely.

Frosted Banana Oatmeal Cookies

Makes about 5 dozen cookies.

¾ cup butter-flavored shortening

1 cup firmly packed brown sugar

1 egg

1 cup mashed ripe banana

1 ½ cups all-purpose flour

1 teaspoon salt

½ teaspoon baking soda

1 teaspoon cinnamon

¼ teaspoon nutmeg

1 ¾ cups quick-cooking oats

½ cup coarsely chopped walnuts

Frosting:

2 tablespoons butter-flavored shortening

¼ cup mashed ripe banana

1 teaspoon lemon juice

2 cups powdered sugar

Preheat oven to 350°F. Grease baking sheets. In a large bowl, with an electric mixer at medium speed, cream together ¾ cup shortening and brown sugar. Beat in egg. Add 1 cup banana and beat until blended. In a medium bowl, stir together flour, salt, baking soda, cinnamon, and nutmeg. Reduce mixer speed to low and mix in flour mixture until blended. Use a spoon to stir in oats and walnuts. Drop by level tablespoonfuls, about 2 inches apart, onto prepared baking sheets. Bake for 15 to 17 minutes or until set. Allow cookies to cool for 1 minute on baking sheets, then transfer to wire racks to cool completely before frosting. Meanwhile, in a medium bowl, with an electric mixer at medium speed, beat 2 tablespoons shortening, ¼ cup banana, and lemon juice. Reduce mixer speed to low. Add powdered sugar, 1 cup at a time, beating well after each addition. Spread each cookie with frosting.

Glazed Pumpkin Cookies

Makes about 3 dozen cookies.

> 2 ½ cups all-purpose flour
>
> 1 teaspoon baking soda
>
> 1 teaspoon baking powder
>
> 1 teaspoon cinnamon
>
> ½ teaspoon nutmeg
>
> ½ teaspoon salt
>
> 1 ½ cups granulated sugar
>
> ½ cup butter or margarine, softened
>
> 1 cup canned pumpkin
>
> 1 egg
>
> 1 teaspoon vanilla extract

Glaze:

> 2 cups powdered sugar
>
> 3 tablespoons milk
>
> 1 tablespoon melted butter or margarine
>
> 1 teaspoon vanilla extract

Preheat oven to 350°F. Grease baking sheets. In a medium bowl, stir together flour, baking soda, baking powder, cinnamon, nutmeg, and salt. In a large bowl, cream together granulated sugar and butter. Beat in pumpkin, egg, and 1 teaspoon vanilla extract until smooth. Gradually beat in flour mixture. Drop by rounded tablespoonfuls onto prepared baking sheets. Bake for 15 to 18 minutes or until edges are firm. Allow cookies to cool for 2 minutes on baking sheets, then transfer to wire racks to cool completely. Meanwhile, in a small bowl, stir together powdered sugar, milk, melted butter, and 1 teaspoon vanilla extract. Stir until smooth. Drizzle cookies with glaze.

Half and Half Cookies

Makes about 5 dozen cookies.

1 ½ cups butter or margarine, softened

½ cup firmly packed brown sugar

¾ cup granulated sugar

3 eggs

3 ¾ cups all-purpose flour

2 teaspoons baking soda

4 squares (4 ounces) bittersweet baking chocolate, chopped, melted, and cooled

1 package (12 ounces) white chips

½ cup chopped pecans

1 package (12 ounces) miniature semi-sweet chocolate chips

Preheat oven to 350°F. In a medium bowl, with an electric mixer at high speed, cream together butter, brown sugar, and granulated sugar. Add eggs, one at a time, beating well after each addition. In a small bowl, combine flour and baking soda. Stir into butter mixture. Equally divide dough into two bowls. Stir bittersweet chocolate, white chips, and pecans into the dough in one bowl. Stir semi-sweet chocolate chips into the second bowl's dough. Scoop a teaspoonful of each dough and drop, side-by-side, onto an ungreased baking sheet to form one cookie. Bake for 8 to 10 minutes or until lightly browned. Transfer to wire racks to cool.

Lolli's Butter Cookies

Makes about 5 dozen cookies.

1 cup butter, no substitutions

⅔ cup granulated sugar

2 eggs, well-beaten

1 ½ cups all-purpose flour

1 teaspoon vanilla extract

Preheat oven to 375°F. Grease baking sheets. Cream butter. Gradually blend in granulated sugar. Stir in eggs, flour, and vanilla extract. Drop by teaspoonfuls onto prepared baking sheets. Bake for 8 minutes. Allow cookies to cool for 1 minute on baking sheets, then transfer to wire racks to cool completely.

Marvelous Maple Drops

Makes about 5 dozen cookies.

 3 cups all-purpose flour

 2 teaspoons baking soda

 2 cups packed brown sugar

 1 cup shortening

 ½ cup butter or margarine, softened

 2 eggs

 1 teaspoon maple flavoring

 1 teaspoon vanilla extract

 1 package (12 ounces) white chips

 ½ cup chopped pecans

 1 cup pecan halves, (about 60)

Frosting:

 4 cups powdered sugar

 4-5 tablespoons milk

 ¼ cup butter or margarine, softened

 1 teaspoon maple flavoring

Preheat oven to 350°F. In a medium bowl, stir together flour and baking soda. In a large bowl, cream together brown sugar, shortening, ½ butter, eggs, 1 teaspoon maple flavoring, and vanilla extract. Gradually beat in flour mixture. Stir in white chips and chopped pecans. Drop by rounded tablespoonfuls onto ungreased baking sheets. Bake for 9 to 12 minutes or until light golden brown. Allow cookies to cool for 2 minutes on baking sheets, then transfer to wire racks to cool completely. Meanwhile, in a medium bowl, stir together powdered sugar, milk, ¼ cup butter, and 1 teaspoon maple flavoring until smooth. Spread each cookie with maple frosting and top with a pecan half.

Mint Chocolate Chip Cookies

Makes about 3 dozen cookies.

> 1 ½ cups semi-sweet chocolate chips, divided
>
> 1 ¾ cups all-purpose flour
>
> ½ teaspoon baking soda
>
> ¼ teaspoon salt
>
> ½ cup butter or margarine, softened
>
> ½ cup granulated sugar
>
> ¼ cup packed brown sugar
>
> ½ teaspoon peppermint extract
>
> ½ teaspoon vanilla extract
>
> 2 eggs
>
> ¾ cup chopped nuts

Preheat oven to 350°F. In a small saucepan, over low heat, melt ¾ cup chocolate chips, stirring until smooth. Set aside to cool. Meanwhile, in a small bowl, stir together flour, baking soda, and salt. In a large bowl, cream together butter, granulated sugar, brown sugar, peppermint extract, and vanilla extract. Add eggs, one at a time, beating well after each addition. Beat in melted chocolate until blended. Gradually beat in flour mixture. Stir in the remaining chocolate chips and nuts. Drop by rounded tablespoonfuls onto ungreased baking sheets. Bake for 8 to 12 minutes or until sides are set. (Centers will still be soft.) Allow cookies to cool for 2 minutes on baking sheets, then transfer to wire racks to cool completely.

Nutty Lemon Drops

Makes about 3 dozen cookies.

1 ½ **cups all-purpose flour**

¾ **teaspoon baking soda**

½ **teaspoon salt**

¾ **cup butter or margarine, softened**

½ **cup packed brown sugar**

¼ **cup granulated sugar**

1 **egg**

1 **tablespoon lemon juice**

1 **package (12 ounces) white chips**

1 **cup coarsely chopped walnuts**

1 **teaspoon grated lemon peel**

Preheat oven to 375°F. In a small bowl, stir together flour, baking soda, and salt. In a large bowl, cream together butter, brown sugar, and granulated sugar. Beat in egg and lemon juice. Gradually beat in flour mixture. Stir in white chips, nuts, and lemon peel. Drop by rounded tablespoonfuls onto ungreased baking sheets. Bake for 7 to 10 minutes or until edges are lightly browned. Allow cookies to cool for 3 minutes on baking sheets, then transfer to wire racks to cool completely.

Oranges and Cream Cookies

Makes about 3 ½ dozen cookies.

2 ¼ cups all-purpose flour

¾ teaspoon baking soda

½ teaspoon salt

1 cup butter or margarine, softened

½ cup granulated sugar

½ cup packed brown sugar

1 egg

2-3 teaspoons grated orange peel

1 package (12 ounces) white chips

Preheat oven to 350°F. In a small bowl, stir together flour, baking soda, and salt. In a large bowl, cream together butter, granulated sugar, and brown sugar. Beat in egg and orange peel. Gradually beat in flour mixture. Stir in white chips. Drop by rounded tablespoonfuls onto ungreased baking sheets. Bake for 10 to 12 minutes or until edges are light golden brown. Allow cookies to cool for 2 minutes on baking sheets, then transfer to wire racks to cool completely.

Peanut Butter-Filled Brownie Thimbles

Makes 1 dozen cookies.

¾ cup granulated sugar

¼ cup butter or margarine, softened

1 tablespoon water

¾ cup semi-sweet chocolate chips

1 egg

½ teaspoon vanilla extract

1 cup all-purpose flour

¼ teaspoon baking soda

1 package (11.5 ounces) milk chocolate chips, divided

¾ cup creamy peanut butter

Preheat oven to 350°F. Grease 12 muffin cups. In medium microwave-safe bowl, cream together granulated sugar, butter, and water. Microwave on HIGH (100% power) for 1 minute or until butter is melted. Add semi-sweet chocolate chips and stir until melted. Stir in egg and vanilla extract. Stir in flour and baking soda. Allow to cool to room temperature before stirring in 1 cup milk chocolate chips. Spoon batter by heaping tablespoonfuls into each muffin cup. Bake for 13 to 15 minutes or until top is set and a toothpick inserted in the center comes out slightly wet. Place pans on wire racks. Meanwhile, add peanut butter to a small bowl. Microwave on HIGH (100% power) for 45 seconds. Remove from microwave and stir. After cookies have cooled slightly, the centers should fall. If they do not, then use the back of a teaspoon to make an indentation. While cookies are still hot, fill each indentation with a scant teaspoonful of peanut butter. Top peanut butter with remaining milk chocolate chips. Allow cookies to cool completely, then gently loosen with a knife and remove from pan.

Root Beer Frosties

Makes about 5 dozen cookies.

1 cup granulated sugar

1 cup packed brown sugar

1 cup butter or margarine, softened

½ cup buttermilk

2 eggs

2 teaspoons root beer extract

1 teaspoon vanilla extract

4 cups all-purpose flour

1 teaspoon baking soda

¼ teaspoon salt

Frosting:

1 cup powdered sugar

1 tablespoon half-and-half

2 teaspoons butter or margarine, softened

1 teaspoon root beer extract

Preheat oven to 375°F. Lightly grease baking sheets. In a large bowl, with an electric mixer at medium speed, beat together granulated sugar, brown sugar, 1 cup butter, buttermilk, eggs, 2 teaspoons root beer extract, and vanilla extract. Beat in flour, baking soda, and salt. Reduce speed to low and continue beating until mixture forms a dough. Drop by rounded tablespoonfuls, about 2 inches apart, onto prepared baking sheets. Bake for 10 to 12 minutes or until set. Allow cookies to cool for 2 minutes on baking sheets, then transfer to wire racks to cool completely before frosting. Meanwhile, in a large bowl, with an electric mixer at low speed, beat frosting ingredients until smooth. Spread each cookie with frosting.

Snow Caps

Makes about 4 ½ dozen cookies.

> 1 ¾ cups all-purpose flour
>
> ½ teaspoon baking soda
>
> ¼ teaspoon salt
>
> ½ cup butter or margarine, softened
>
> ¾ cup granulated sugar
>
> 1 egg
>
> ½ teaspoon vanilla extract
>
> ½ cup sour cream
>
> ¾ cup sweetened dried cranberries
>
> ¾ cup white chips
>
> ¾ cup semi-sweet chocolate chips
>
> ¾ cup chopped pecans

Glaze:

> 2 cups powdered sugar
>
> 8 teaspoons milk

Preheat oven to 375°F. Grease baking sheets. In a medium bowl, combine flour, baking soda, and salt. In a large mixing bowl, with an electric mixer at medium speed, cream together butter and granulated sugar. Beat in egg and vanilla extract just until combined. With electric mixer at low speed, gradually add dry ingredients alternately with sour cream, beating after each addition, until blended. Stir in cranberries, white chips, semi-sweet chocolate chips, and pecans. Drop by rounded teaspoonfuls onto prepared baking sheets. Bake for 8 to 10 minutes or until set and lightly browned around edges. Allow cookies to cool for 1 minute on baking sheets, then transfer to wire racks to cool completely. Meanwhile, in a small bowl, add powdered sugar and gradually mix in enough milk for desired glazing consistency. Dip tops of cookies into glaze. Place cookies upright on sheets of wax paper and let stand until glaze is set.

Sweet Graham Scotchies

Makes about 4 dozen cookies.

2 cups graham cracker crumbs

1 ½ cups all-purpose flour

1 teaspoon baking soda

½ teaspoon salt

1 cup butter or margarine, softened

¾ cup granulated sugar

¾ cup firmly packed brown sugar

2 eggs

1 teaspoon vanilla extract

1 package (11 ounces) butterscotch chips

Preheat oven to 350°F. In a small bowl, stir together graham cracker crumbs, flour, baking soda, and salt. In a large bowl, cream together butter, granulated sugar, and brown sugar. Beat in eggs and vanilla extract. Gradually beat in flour mixture. Stir in butterscotch chips. Drop by rounded tablespoonfuls onto ungreased baking sheets. Bake for 9 to 11 minutes or until set. Allow cookies to cool for 2 minutes on baking sheets, then transfer to wire racks to cool completely.

Toffee Drop Cookies

Makes about 6 dozen cookies.

1 cup butter or margarine, softened

1 cup granulated sugar

1 cup packed brown sugar

½ teaspoon salt

3 eggs

1 teaspoon vanilla extract

3 ½ cups all-purpose flour

2 teaspoons baking soda

2 teaspoons cream of tartar

1 ⅓ cups toffee baking bits

Preheat oven to 350°F. Lightly grease baking sheets. In a large bowl, cream together butter, granulated sugar, brown sugar, and salt until blended. Add eggs and vanilla extract. Beat well. In a large bowl, combine flour, baking soda, and cream of tartar. Gradually add to the butter mixture, beating after each addition, until blended. Stir in toffee bits. Drop by heaping teaspoonfuls onto prepared baking sheets. Bake for 8 to 10 minutes or until lightly browned. Allow cookies to cool for 2 minutes on baking sheets, then transfer to wire racks to cool completely.

Tropical Bliss White Chip Cookies

Makes about 3 dozen cookies.

1 ⅔ cups all-purpose flour

¾ teaspoon baking powder

½ teaspoon baking soda

½ teaspoon salt

¾ cup butter or margarine, softened

¾ cup packed brown sugar

⅓ cup granulated sugar

1 teaspoon vanilla extract

1 egg

1 package (12 ounces) white chips

1 cup flaked coconut

¾ cup chopped macadamia nuts or walnuts

Preheat oven to 375°F. In a small bowl, stir together flour, baking powder, baking soda, and salt. In a large bowl, cream together butter, brown sugar, granulated sugar, and vanilla extract. Beat in egg. Gradually beat in flour mixture. Stir in white chips, coconut, and nuts. Drop by rounded tablespoonfuls onto ungreased baking sheets. Bake for 8 to 11 minutes or until edges are lightly browned. Allow cookies to cool for 2 minutes on baking sheets, then transfer to wire racks to cool completely.

White Chip P-Nutties

Makes about 3 dozen cookies.

> 2 ¼ cups all-purpose flour
>
> 1 teaspoon baking powder
>
> 1 teaspoon baking soda
>
> 1 teaspoon salt
>
> 1 ½ cups creamy peanut butter
>
> 1 cup butter or margarine, softened
>
> 1 cup granulated sugar
>
> 1 cup firmly packed brown sugar
>
> 1 teaspoon vanilla extract
>
> 2 eggs, slightly beaten
>
> 1 package (12 ounces) white chips
>
> 1 ⅓ cups walnuts, coarsely chopped

Preheat oven to 350°F. In a small bowl, stir together flour, baking powder, baking soda, and salt. In a large bowl, with an electric mixer at medium speed, cream together peanut butter, butter, granulated sugar, brown sugar, and vanilla extract. Add eggs and mix until well blended. Gradually beat in flour mixture. Stir in white chips and nuts. Drop by rounded tablespoonfuls onto ungreased baking sheets. Bake for 15 to 16 minutes. Allow cookies to cool for 5 minutes on baking sheets, then transfer to wire racks to cool completely.

White Chocolate Chunk Cranberry Cookies

Makes about 6 dozen cookies.

1 cup butter or margarine, softened

1 cup granulated sugar

½ cup firmly packed brown sugar

2 eggs

1 teaspoon vanilla extract

2 ¼ cups all-purpose flour

1 teaspoon baking soda

½ teaspoon salt

12 squares (12 ounces) premium white baking chocolate, chopped

2 cups chopped pecans

2 cups dried cranberries

Preheat oven to 375°F. In a large bowl, with an electric mixer at medium speed, cream together butter, granulated sugar, and brown sugar. Beat in eggs and vanilla extract. Add flour, baking soda, and salt. Mix until well blended. Stir in white chocolate, pecans, and cranberries. Drop by rounded tablespoonfuls onto ungreased baking sheets. Bake for 9 to 11 minutes or until lightly browned. Allow cookies to cool for 3 minutes on baking sheets, then transfer to wire racks to cool completely.

Buttercrunch Bars

Makes 16 bars.

1 cup crunchy peanut butter

½ cup granulated sugar

½ cup dark corn syrup

1 teaspoon vanilla extract

3 cups cornflakes, crushed

1 cup semi-sweet chocolate chips, melted

Lightly butter a 9x9x2-inch baking pan. In a medium saucepan, over medium heat, combine peanut butter, granulated sugar, and corn syrup. Heat to boiling, stirring frequently. Remove from heat and stir in vanilla extract. Add cereal and stir until well coated. Gently press mixture into prepared baking pan. Spread melted chocolate evenly over top. Refrigerate for 1 hour or until chocolate has hardened. Cut into bars.

Candy Bar Crispies

Makes 36 bars.

½ cup butter or margarine

1 bag (10.5 ounces) miniature marshmallows

6 cups crisped rice cereal

3 chocolate-covered caramel and nougat candy bars (2.05 ounces each), chopped, divided (Refrigerate candy bars for 1 hour prior to cutting for easier chopping.)

Grease a 13x9x2-inch baking pan. In a medium saucepan, melt butter over medium-low heat. Add marshmallows and stir until melted. Remove from heat. Fold in cereal. Stir in 1 cup of the chopped candy. Candy will melt slightly. Gently press mixture into prepared baking pan. Sprinkle remaining chopped candy over top. Cut into bars.

Caramel Nut Bars

Makes 36 bars.

4 cups powdered sugar

1 ½ cups graham cracker crumbs

1 ½ cups creamy peanut butter

1 ½ cups slivered almonds, chopped, divided

¾ cup butter or margarine, melted

1 package (14 ounces) caramels, unwrapped

¼ cup water

6 squares (6 ounces) semi-sweet baking chocolate, chopped

3 tablespoons butter or margarine

In a large bowl, stir together powdered sugar, graham cracker crumbs, peanut butter, 1 cup almonds, and melted butter. Firmly press mixture into the bottom of a 13x9x2-inch baking pan. Add caramels and water to a large saucepan and cook over low heat, stirring frequently, until caramels have completely melted and mixture is well blended. Pour melted caramels over crust. Add chocolate and 3 tablespoons butter to a large saucepan and cook over low heat, stirring frequently, until chocolate has completely melted and mixture is well blended. Spread over caramel layer, then sprinkle reserved almonds over chocolate layer and gently press them into place. Refrigerate for at least 1 hour before cutting into bars. Store, covered, in the refrigerator.

Chewy Cereal Bars

Makes 72 bars.

9 cups crisped rice cereal

6 ½ cups quick-cooking oats

1 cup cornflakes

1 cup flaked coconut

2 packages (one 16 ounces, one 10.5 ounces) miniature marshmallows

1 cup butter or margarine

½ cup honey

½ cup semi-sweet chocolate chips

½ cup raisins

½ cup miniature candy-coated chocolate baking bits

Butter two 15x10x1-inch baking pans. In a large bowl, toss together crisped rice cereal, oats, cornflakes, and coconut. In a large saucepan, over low heat, cook and stir marshmallows and butter until melted and smooth. Add honey and stir until blended. Pour marshmallow mixture over cereal mixture. Stir to coat. Allow to cool for 5 minutes. Stir in chocolate chips, raisins, and candy-coated chocolate baking bits. Press into prepared baking pans. Allow to cool for 30 minutes before cutting into bars.

Chewy Chocolate Coconut Cookies

Makes about 3 dozen cookies.

> **1 cup semi-sweet chocolate chips**
>
> **5 tablespoons butter or margarine**
>
> **16 large marshmallows**
>
> **1 teaspoon vanilla extract**
>
> **2 cups quick-cooking or old-fashioned oats**
>
> **1 cup shredded coconut**

Line baking sheets with wax paper. In a large saucepan, over low heat, melt chocolate chips, butter, and marshmallows, stirring constantly, until smooth. Remove from heat and allow to cool slightly. Add vanilla extract and stir. Stir in oats and coconut. Drop by rounded teaspoonfuls onto prepared baking sheets. Cover and refrigerate for 2 to 3 hours or until firm. Before serving, let cookies stand at room temperature for about 15 minutes. Store in the refrigerator in a tightly covered container.

Chewy Chocolatey Butterscotch Bars

Makes 30 bars.

1 ½ **cups creamy peanut butter**

1 **cup granulated sugar**

1 **cup light corn syrup**

6 **cups crisped rice cereal**

1 **package (11 ounces) butterscotch chips**

1 **cup semi-sweet chocolate chips**

Coat a 13x9x2-inch pan with cooking spray. In a large saucepan, stir together peanut butter, granulated sugar, and corn syrup. Cook over medium-low heat, stirring frequently, until melted. Remove from heat. Add cereal and stir until completely coated. Press mixture into bottom of prepared pan. In microwave, melt butterscotch and semi-sweet chocolate chips. Stir until smooth. Spread over bottom cereal layer. Refrigerate for 15 to 20 minutes before cutting into bars.

Chocolate-Covered Cherry Cookies

Makes about 2 ½ dozen cookies.

> **2 cups granulated sugar**
>
> **½ cup milk**
>
> **¼ cup butter or margarine**
>
> **⅓ cup unsweetened cocoa**
>
> **1 teaspoon vanilla extract**
>
> **½ cup creamy peanut butter**
>
> **1 jar (10 ounces) maraschino cherries, drained and chopped**
>
> **3 cups quick-cooking oats**

In a large saucepan, over medium-high heat, combine granulated sugar, milk, butter, and unsweetened cocoa. Heat to a rolling boil. Continue boiling for 1 minute. Remove from heat. Stir in vanilla extract. Add peanut butter and stir until melted. Stir in cherries and oats. Drop by tablespoonfuls onto sheets of wax paper and allow cookies to set.

Chocolate Toffee Drops

Makes about 1 ½ dozen cookies.

½ cup unsalted butter

¼ cup unsweetened cocoa

2 cups granulated sugar

½ cup milk

1 ½ teaspoons vanilla extract

3 ½ cups quick-cooking oats

1 cup toffee baking bits

In a large saucepan, over medium-high heat, combine butter, unsweetened cocoa, granulated sugar, and milk. Heat to a soft boil. Remove from heat and stir in vanilla extract. Stir in oats and toffee bits. Drop by tablespoonfuls onto sheets of wax paper and allow cookies to set.

Chocolate-Topped Peanut Butter Bars

Makes 48 bars.

½ cup butter or margarine, melted

2 cups powdered sugar

1 ½ cups graham cracker crumbs

1 cup creamy peanut butter

12 squares (12 ounces) semi-sweet baking chocolate, melted and slightly cooled

Line a 13x9x2-inch baking pan with aluminum foil allowing ends to extend over the two sides of the pan. In a large bowl, stir together melted butter, powdered sugar, graham cracker crumbs, and peanut butter. Spread mixture into the bottom of prepared pan. Pour melted chocolate over the bottom layer. Cool before partially cutting into squares. Refrigerate for 1 hour. Remove from refrigerator. Use excess aluminum foil to lift contents from the pan. Remove the aluminum foil and finish cutting into squares.

Monkey Bars

Makes 12 bars.

1 cup coarsely chopped walnuts

¼ cup flaked coconut

¼ cup butter or margarine

1 bag (10 ounces) marshmallows

2 tablespoons unsweetened cocoa

6 cups chocolate-flavored cereal puffs

1 cup coarsely crushed dried banana chips

Preheat oven to 350°F. Lightly grease a 13x9x2-inch baking pan. Toast walnuts on an ungreased baking sheet with sides for 5 minutes. Remove from oven and toss coconut into walnuts. Return to oven and continue baking, stirring twice, for an additional 4 to 6 minutes or until coconut is light golden brown. Set aside until cool. Meanwhile, in a large saucepan, melt butter over medium heat. Stir in marshmallows. Cook, stirring constantly, for 4 to 6 minutes or until melted. Add cocoa and stir until well blended. Remove from heat. Fold in cereal, banana chips, toasted walnuts, and coconut until well coated. Lightly press mixture into prepared baking pan. Transfer pan to a wire rack and allow cookies to cool for 30 minutes before cutting into bars.

Peanut Butter and Jelly Bars

Makes 32 bars.

3 cups miniature marshmallows

1 cup crunchy peanut butter

½ cup butter or margarine

4 ½ cups crisped rice cereal

Filling:

⅔ cup strawberry jam

Topping:

½ cup milk chocolate chips

1 tablespoon crunchy peanut butter

2 teaspoons shortening

In a medium saucepan, over low heat, melt marshmallows, 1 cup peanut butter, and butter, stirring constantly, until smooth. Quickly stir in cereal until well coated. Press into an ungreased 11x7x2-inch baking pan. Drop teaspoonfuls of jam over hot cereal mixture. Carefully spread over top. In a small saucepan, over low heat, melt chocolate chips, 1 tablespoon peanut butter, and shortening, stirring occasionally, until smooth. Carefully spread over jam layer. Refrigerate for 2 hours or until the chocolate layer is firm. Cut into bars.

Peanut Butter Crunchies

Makes about 2 ½ dozen cookies.

¼ **cup packed brown sugar**

¼ **cup granulated sugar**

½ **cup light corn syrup**

¾ **cup creamy peanut butter**

1 **teaspoon vanilla extract**

2 ½ **cups crisped rice cereal**

Combine brown sugar, granulated sugar, and corn syrup in a small saucepan. Bring mixture to a boil. Remove from heat. Stir in peanut butter and vanilla extract until well mixed. Fold in cereal until well coated. Drop by rounded tablespoonfuls onto waxed paper.

White Chocolate Munchers

Makes 24 bars.

> **2 cups crisped rice cereal**
>
> **2 cups peanut butter-flavored corn and oat cereal**
>
> **2 cups miniature marshmallows**
>
> **2 cups chopped pecans**
>
> **1 ½ pounds white chocolate, chopped**

Coat a 13x9x2-inch baking pan with cooking spray. In a large bowl, toss together crisped rice cereal, peanut butter-flavored corn and oat cereal, marshmallows, and pecans. In a medium bowl, microwave chocolate on HIGH (100% power) for about 3 minutes, stirring halfway through. Remove from microwave and stir until smooth. Add melted chocolate to cereal mixture and stir until coated. Spread into prepared baking pan. Refrigerate for about 1 hour or until firm. Cut into bars.

Rolled Cookies

Butterscotchy Cutouts

Makes about 4 dozen cookies.

1 cup butterscotch chips

3 cups all-purpose flour

1 cup butter or margarine, softened

½ cup granulated sugar

½ cup firmly packed brown sugar

1 egg

2 tablespoons milk

2 teaspoons vanilla extract

Colored decorator sugar

Preheat oven to 375°F. In a small saucepan, over low heat, melt butterscotch chips, stirring constantly, until smooth. Pour melted chips into a large bowl. Add all of the remaining ingredients except for the decorator sugar. With an electric mixer at low speed, beat until well mixed. Divide cookie dough in half. Slightly flatten halves. Wrap each half in plastic food wrap and refrigerate for 1 hour or until firm. Working with one-half at a time, roll out dough, on a lightly floured surface, to ⅛-inch thickness. Using 2 ½-inch cookie cutters, cut into desired shapes. Place 1 inch apart on ungreased baking sheets. Sprinkle with decorator sugar. Bake for 5 to 8 minutes or until lightly browned at edges. Transfer to wire racks to cool.

Crispy Coffee Cutouts

Makes about 3 dozen cookies.

¼ cup hot water

1 tablespoon instant coffee granules

1 cup butter or margarine, softened

1 cup granulated sugar

1 egg

2 ½ cups all-purpose flour

1 teaspoon baking powder

Preheat oven to 400°F. In a small bowl, stir hot water and coffee granules until coffee granules are dissolved. In a large bowl, cream together butter and granulated sugar. Add egg, and with an electric mixer at medium speed, beat until creamy. Beat in coffee, scraping sides of bowl often, until well blended. Add flour and baking powder. With electric mixer at low speed, beat, scraping bowl often, until well mixed. Divide dough into thirds. Shape dough into 3 balls. Wrap each ball in plastic food wrap and flatten each to ½-inch thickness. Chill for 2 to 3 hours. On a lightly floured surface, one-third at a time, roll dough to ¼-inch thickness. Cut out shapes using cookie cutters. Place 1 inch apart on ungreased baking sheets. Bake for 6 to 10 minutes or lightly browned on edges. Transfer to wire racks to cool.

Favorite Cream Cheese Cutouts

Makes about 5 dozen cookies.

> **1 cup granulated sugar**
>
> **1 cup butter or margarine, softened**
>
> **1 package (3 ounces) cream cheese, softened**
>
> **1 teaspoon vanilla extract**
>
> **1 egg**
>
> **2 ½ cups all-purpose flour**
>
> **¼ teaspoon salt**
>
> **Colored decorator sugar**

Preheat oven to 375°F. In a large bowl, with an electric mixer at medium speed, beat granulated sugar, butter, and cream cheese until light and fluffy. Blend in vanilla extract and egg. Add flour and salt. Beat until well mixed. Wrap in plastic food wrap and refrigerate for 1 to 2 hours. On a lightly floured surface, working with one-half of the dough at a time, roll out to ⅛-inch thickness. Cut into desired shapes with 2 ½-inch cookie cutters. Place 1 inch apart on ungreased baking sheets. Sprinkle with decorator sugar. Bake for 7 to 10 minutes or until light golden brown at edges. Allow cookies to cool for 1 minute on baking sheets, then transfer to wire racks to cool completely.

Minty Chocolate Cutouts

Makes about 4 dozen cookies.

1 cup butter or margarine, softened

1 cup granulated sugar

1 egg

1 teaspoon vanilla extract

½ teaspoon peppermint extract

2 cups all-purpose flour

½ cup unsweetened cocoa

½ teaspoon baking soda

¼ teaspoon salt

Frosting:

2 cups powdered sugar

¼ cup butter or margarine, softened

½ teaspoon peppermint extract

1-2 tablespoons milk

Preheat oven to 400°F. In a large bowl, combine 1 cup butter, granulated sugar, egg, vanilla extract, and ½ teaspoon peppermint extract. With an electric mixer at medium speed, beat until creamy. Add flour, cocoa, baking soda, and salt. With electric mixer at low speed, beat until well mixed. Divide dough in half. Shape each half into a ½-inch-thick circle. Wrap each circle in plastic food wrap and refrigerate for 1 hour or until firm. Working with one-half at a time, roll out dough on a lightly floured surface to ⅛-inch thickness. Using 2 ½-inch cookie cutters, cut into desired shapes. Place cookies 1 inch apart on ungreased baking sheets. Bake for 6 to 8 minutes or until cookies are set. Allow cookies to cool for 1 minute on baking sheets, then transfer to wire racks to cool completely before frosting. Meanwhile, in a small bowl, combine powdered sugar, ¼ cup butter, and ½ teaspoon peppermint extract. With an electric mixer at low speed, beat, gradually adding enough milk, until desired spreading consistency. Spread each cookie with frosting.

Pecan Sugar Cookies

Makes about 3 ½ dozen cookies.

3 ¾ cups all-purpose flour

1 ½ teaspoons baking powder

¼ teaspoon salt

1 cup shortening

1 ½ cups granulated sugar

2 eggs

2 teaspoons vanilla extract

1 cup pecans, finely chopped

Colored decorator sugar

Preheat oven to 375°F. Lightly grease baking sheets. In a large bowl, stir together flour, baking powder, and salt. In another large bowl, cream together shortening and granulated sugar. Add eggs, one at a time, beating well after each addition. Beat in vanilla extract. Gradually blend in flour mixture. Fold in pecans. Roll out dough, on a floured surface, to a thickness of ⅛-inch. Cut into desired shapes with 2 to 2 ½-inch cookie cutters. Place cookies 1 inch apart on prepared baking sheets. Sprinkle with decorator sugar. Bake for 8 to 10 minutes or until edges are very lightly browned. Transfer to wire racks to cool. (For softer cookies, roll the dough out to a thickness of ¼-inch and increase the baking time to 10 to 12 minutes.)

Reach for the Stars Cookies

Makes about 5 dozen cookies.

1 cup granulated sugar

½ cup butter or margarine, softened

½ cup sour cream

1 egg

2 teaspoons freshly grated orange peel

1 teaspoon vanilla extract

½ teaspoon orange extract

2 ½ cups all-purpose flour

¾ teaspoon baking powder

¼ teaspoon baking soda

¼ teaspoon salt

2-3 drops yellow food color

2-3 drops red food color

Large grain sugar

Preheat oven to 375°F. In a large bowl, with an electric mixer at medium speed, cream together granulated sugar and butter. Beat in sour cream, egg, orange peel, vanilla extract, and orange extract until well mixed. Add flour, baking powder, baking soda, and salt. With electric mixer at low speed beat until well mixed. Divide dough into three equal portions. Stir yellow food color into one-third of dough and red food color into second third. Leave the final third untinted. Wrap each portion in plastic food wrap and refrigerate for 1 hour or until firm. Tear each portion of dough in half and randomly spoon 1 to 1 ½-inch chunks of each color of dough onto a lightly floured surface. Keep remaining dough refrigerated until needed. Press chunks of dough together to form a circle. Roll out to ¼-inch thickness. Cut into star shapes with 2 to 2 ½-inch cookie cutters. Repeat the process with the remaining dough. Place cookies 2 inches apart on ungreased baking sheets. Sprinkle large grain sugar over tops of cookies before baking. Bake for 5 to 7 minutes or until lightly browned around edges. Transfer to wire racks to cool.

Soft Sugar Cookies

Makes about 6 dozen cookies.

4 cups all-purpose flour, divided

2 cups granulated sugar

1 cup butter or margarine, softened

½ cup sour cream

2 eggs

1 tablespoon baking powder

1 teaspoon baking soda

1 teaspoon vanilla extract

½ teaspoon salt

Colored decorator sugar

Preheat oven to 350°F. In a large bowl, combine 2 cups of the flour, granulated sugar, butter, sour cream, eggs, baking powder, baking soda, vanilla extract, and salt. With an electric mixer at low speed, beat until well mixed. Gradually stir in remaining flour. Divide dough into four equal portions. Wrap each portion in plastic food wrap and refrigerate for 2 hours. On a well-floured surface, roll out dough to ⅛-inch thickness. Using 2 ½-inch cookie cutters, cut into desired shapes. Place cookies 1 inch apart on ungreased baking sheets. Sprinkle with decorator sugar. Bake for 7 to 10 minutes or until lightly browned at edges. Transfer to wire racks to cool.

Caramel-Surprise Chocolate Cookies

Makes about 5 dozen cookies.

1 cup butter, softened (no substitutions)

1 cup plus 1 tablespoon granulated sugar, divided

1 cup firmly packed brown sugar

2 eggs

1 teaspoon vanilla extract

2 ½ cups all-purpose flour

¾ cup unsweetened cocoa

1 teaspoon baking soda

1 ¼ cups chopped pecans, divided

1 package (13 ounces) foil wrapped, chocolate-covered, caramel candies, unwrapped

4 squares (4 ounces) white baking chocolate, melted

Preheat oven to 375°F. Grease baking sheets. In a large bowl, with an electric mixer at medium speed, cream together butter, 1 cup granulated sugar, and brown sugar. Add eggs, one at a time, beating well after each addition. Beat in vanilla extract. In a medium bowl, stir together flour, cocoa, and baking soda. Gradually beat flour mixture into butter mixture. Stir in ½ cup pecans. In a small bowl, stir together 1 tablespoon granulated sugar and ¾ cup pecans. Shape a tablespoonful of dough around each piece of candy. Once candy is well sealed and completely covered, shape dough into a ball. Press one-half of each ball into the pecan mixture. Place balls, nut-side-up, about 2 inches apart on prepared baking sheets. Bake for 7 to 10 minutes or until cookies are set and tops are slightly cracked. Allow cookies to cool for 2 minutes on baking sheets, then transfer to wire racks to cool completely. Drizzle melted white chocolate over cooled cookies.

Chewy Molasses Crinkles

Makes about 4 dozen cookies.

> ¾ cup shortening
>
> 1 cup packed brown sugar
>
> ¼ cup mild-flavor molasses
>
> 1 egg
>
> 2 ¼ cups all-purpose flour
>
> 2 teaspoons baking soda
>
> 1 teaspoon cinnamon
>
> 1 teaspoon ginger
>
> ½ teaspoon cloves
>
> ¼ teaspoon salt
>
> Granulated sugar

Preheat oven to 375°F. Lightly grease baking sheets. In a large bowl, thoroughly mix shortening, brown sugar, molasses, and egg. Gradually add flour, stirring after each addition. Stir in baking soda, cinnamon, ginger, cloves, and salt until well mixed. Refrigerate, in a covered bowl, for at least 2 hours. Shape dough into 1 ¼-inch balls. Dip tops of balls in granulated sugar. Place 3 inches apart, with sugared sides up, on prepared baking sheets. Sprinkle each cookie with 2 to 3 drops of water before baking. Bake just until set but not hard; about 10 to 12 minutes. Transfer to wire racks to cool.

Chocolate Crinkle-Top Cookies

Makes about 6 dozen cookies.

½ cup vegetable oil

4 squares (4 ounces) unsweetened baking chocolate, melted and cooled

2 cups granulated sugar

2 teaspoons vanilla extract

4 eggs

2 cups all-purpose flour

2 teaspoons baking powder

½ teaspoon salt

½ cup powdered sugar

Preheat oven to 350°F. Grease baking sheets. In a large bowl, combine oil, chocolate, granulated sugar, and vanilla extract. Stir in eggs, one at a time. Mix in flour, baking powder, and salt. Refrigerate, covered, for at least 3 hours. Shape dough into 1-inch balls. Pour powdered sugar in a shallow bowl. Place balls in powdered sugar and roll until coated completely. Arrange balls about 2 inches apart on prepared baking sheets. Bake for 10 to 12 minutes. Transfer to wire racks to cool.

Chocolate-Kissed Almond Cookies

Makes about 2 dozen cookies.

½ cup butter or margarine, softened

½ cup granulated sugar

1 egg

1 teaspoon almond extract

1 ⅓ cups all-purpose flour

1 teaspoon baking soda

½ cup finely chopped, toasted, slivered almonds

24 foil-wrapped milk chocolate candies, unwrapped

Preheat oven to 350°F. In a large bowl, with an electric mixer at medium speed, cream together butter and granulated sugar. Beat in egg and almond extract. Add flour and baking soda. Beat until well blended. Shape dough into 1-inch balls. Roll balls in almonds, then place on ungreased baking sheets. Bake for 7 to 9 minutes or until lightly browned. Remove from oven and immediately press 1 piece of candy, lightly, into the center of each cookie. Transfer to wire racks to cool.

Deluxe Chocolate Chip Cookies

Makes about 7 ½ dozen cookies.

1 cup butter or margarine, softened

2 cups firmly packed brown sugar

2 eggs

1 teaspoon vanilla extract

2 cups all-purpose flour

½ teaspoon baking powder

2 cups crisped rice cereal

2 cups semi-sweet chocolate chips

1 cup sweetened flaked coconut

1 cup chopped walnuts or pecans

Preheat oven to 350°F. Lightly grease baking sheets. In a large bowl, with an electric mixer at low speed, cream together butter and brown sugar until light and fluffy. Add eggs and vanilla extract. Beat until well mixed. In a medium bowl, combine flour and baking powder. Gradually add to creamed mixture, beating after each addition, until mixed. Stir in cereal, chocolate chips, coconut, and nuts. Shape dough into 1-inch balls and place on prepared baking sheets. Bake for 10 to 12 minutes or until lightly browned. Transfer to wire racks to cool.

Fin Mints

Makes about 3 ½ dozen cookies.

1 cup butter or margarine, softened

1 ½ cups granulated sugar, divided

½ cup firmly packed brown sugar

1 egg

1 teaspoon peppermint extract

1 teaspoon vanilla extract

2 cups all-purpose flour

⅓ cup unsweetened cocoa

½ teaspoon baking powder

½ teaspoon salt

21 crème de menthe thin candy rectangles, unwrapped, cut in half diagonally

Preheat oven to 350°F. In a large bowl, cream together butter, 1 cup granulated sugar, and brown sugar. Add egg, peppermint extract, and vanilla extract. With an electric mixer at medium speed, beat until well mixed. Add flour, cocoa, baking powder, and salt. With electric mixer at low speed, beat until well mixed. Shape dough into 1-inch balls. Roll balls in remaining granulated sugar. Place on ungreased baking sheets. Bake for 10 to 13 minutes or until cookies are set. Immediately press a candy half, pointed side up, into the center of each cookie. Allow cookies to cool for 2 minutes on baking sheets, then transfer to wire racks to cool completely.

Frosty Pink Lemonade Cookies

Makes about 4 ½ dozen cookies.

1 cup granulated sugar, divided

¼ cup butter or margarine, softened

1 egg

2 teaspoons freshly grated lemon peel

1 teaspoon lemon juice

1-2 drops red food color

1 cup all-purpose flour

½ teaspoon baking powder

¼ teaspoon salt

Powdered sugar

Preheat oven to 400°F. Lightly grease baking sheets. In a large bowl, combine ½ cup granulated sugar, butter, egg, lemon peel, lemon juice, and red food color. With an electric mixer at medium speed, beat, scraping bowl often, until creamy. Add flour, baking powder, and salt. With electric mixer at low speed, beat until well mixed. Wrap in plastic food wrap and refrigerate for 1 hour or until firm. Shape dough into ½-inch balls and roll in remaining granulated sugar. Place on prepared baking sheets. With the bottom of a buttered glass dipped in sugar, flatten balls to ¼-inch thickness. Bake for 5 to 7 minutes or until edges are lightly browned. Sprinkle with powdered sugar while still warm. Transfer to wire racks to cool.

Fudge Thimbles

Makes about 4 dozen cookies.

½ cup butter or margarine, softened

½ cup creamy peanut butter

½ cup granulated sugar

½ cup packed brown sugar

1 egg

½ teaspoon vanilla extract

1 ¼ cups all-purpose flour

¾ teaspoon baking soda

½ teaspoon salt

Fudge Filling:

1 cup milk chocolate chips

1 cup semi-sweet chocolate chips

1 can (14 ounces) sweetened condensed milk

1 teaspoon vanilla extract

¾ cup pecan halves

Preheat oven to 325°F. Lightly grease mini-muffin pans. In a large bowl, cream together butter, peanut butter, granulated sugar, and brown sugar. Stir in egg and ½ teaspoon vanilla extract. In a small bowl, combine flour, baking soda, and salt. Stir dry ingredients into creamed mixture. Chill for 1 hour. Shape dough into 1-inch balls. Place one ball in each mini-muffin pan section. Bake for 14 to 16 minutes or until lightly browned. Remove from oven. Immediately make an indentation in the center by pressing each cookie with a melon baller. Allow cookies to cool for 5 minutes, then gently loosen with a knife and remove from pans. Transfer to wire racks to cool completely. Meanwhile, place milk chocolate and semi-sweet chocolate chips in a double boiler over simmering water. Mix in sweetened condensed milk and 1 teaspoon vanilla extract. Use a small pitcher to fill each indentation with fudge filling. Top filling with a pecan half.

Molasses Oatmeal Crackles

Makes about 3 ½ dozen cookies.

1 ¼ cups all-purpose flour

1 cup quick-cooking oats

2 teaspoons baking soda

2 teaspoons ginger

1 teaspoon cinnamon

½ teaspoon cloves

½ teaspoon salt

1 cup firmly packed brown sugar

⅓ cup butter or margarine, melted

¼ cup unsweetened applesauce

¼ cup molasses

1 egg, lightly beaten

½ cup granulated sugar

Preheat oven to 375°F. Lightly grease baking sheets. In a medium bowl, stir together flour, oats, baking soda, ginger, cinnamon, cloves, and salt. In a large bowl, mix brown sugar, butter, applesauce, molasses, and egg until well blended. Add flour mixture and mix well. Cover and chill for at least 1 hour. Shape dough into 1-inch balls. Roll each ball in granulated sugar. Place on prepared baking sheets. Bake for 7 to 9 minutes or until tops become crackled. Allow cookies to cool for 2 minutes on baking sheets, then transfer to wire racks to cool completely.

Moo Cow Cookies

Makes about 5 dozen cookies.

1 ½ cups butter or margarine, softened

¾ cup powdered sugar

1 tablespoon vanilla extract

½ teaspoon salt

3 cups all-purpose flour

1 package (12 ounces) miniature semi-sweet chocolate chips

½ cup finely chopped nuts

Powdered sugar

Preheat oven to 375°F. In a large bowl, cream together butter, powdered sugar, vanilla extract, and salt. Gradually beat in flour. Stir in chocolate chips and nuts. Measure dough into level tablespoons. Shape dough into 1 ¼-inch balls and place on ungreased baking sheets. Bake for 10 to 12 minutes or until lightly browned. Sprinkle powdered sugar over hot cookies. Allow cookies to cool for 10 minutes on baking sheets, then transfer to wire racks to cool completely. After cookies have cooled completely, roll in additional powdered sugar.

Peanut Butter and Chocolate Chippers

Makes 3 dozen cookies.

¾ cup butter or margarine, softened

⅓ cup granulated sugar

1 ½ cups all-purpose flour

1 package (11 ounces) peanut butter and milk chocolate chips, divided

2 eggs

1 can (14 ounces) sweetened condensed milk

1 teaspoon vanilla extract

Preheat oven to 350°F. Heavily grease 36 mini-muffin cups. In a small bowl, cream together butter and granulated sugar. Add flour and beat until mixture is moist and crumbly. Shape rounded teaspoonfuls of dough into balls. Press one ball into the bottom and halfway up the sides of each muffin cup. Place 3 peanut butter and 3 chocolate chips in each cup. In a medium bowl, beat eggs with a wire whisk. Stir in sweetened condensed milk and vanilla extract. Spoon mixture into each muffin cup, filling almost to the top. Bake for 15 to 18 minutes or until centers are puffy and edges have just started to brown. Place mini-muffin pans on wire racks. Use a knife to gently loosen edges of cookies from pan. Allow centers to flatten. Top warm cookies with half of the remaining chips. Top cookies again with the rest of the remaining chips. Allow cookies to cool completely, then gently loosen with a knife and remove from pans.

Peanut Butter Mud Puddles

Makes 2 ½ dozen cookies.

½ cup creamy peanut butter

½ cup butter or margarine, softened

½ cup granulated sugar

½ cup firmly packed brown sugar

1 egg, beaten

½ teaspoon vanilla extract

1 ¼ cups all-purpose flour

¾ teaspoon baking soda

½ teaspoon salt

36 miniature peanut butter cups, unwrapped

Preheat oven to 375°F. In a large bowl, cream together peanut butter, butter, granulated sugar, and brown sugar. Add egg, vanilla extract, flour, baking soda, and salt. Stir until well mixed. Shape dough into 1-inch balls. Place balls in mini-muffin pans. Bake for 8 to 10 minutes. Immediately after removing muffin pans from oven, gently press 1 peanut butter cup into the center of each cookie. Transfer pans to wire racks and allow cookies to cool completely before removing from pans.

Pecan Jewels

Makes about 3 dozen cookies.

½ cup packed brown sugar

1 cup shortening

3 eggs, separated

1 ½ teaspoons vanilla extract

¼ teaspoon salt

2 cups all-purpose flour

2 cups finely chopped pecans

1 cup preserves or jam, any flavor

Preheat oven to 350°F. Lightly grease baking sheets. In a large bowl, cream together brown sugar, shortening, egg yolks, vanilla extract, and salt. Gradually add flour and stir until well blended. In a small bowl, use a fork to beat the egg whites until foamy. Place pecans in a separate small bowl. Shape dough into 1-inch balls. Dip each ball into the egg whites. Roll in pecans and place on prepared baking sheets. Using your thumb, make an indentation centered in the top of each cookie. Bake for 8 minutes. Remove from oven. Fill each indentation with a teaspoonful of jam. Return to oven and bake for an additional 6 to 9 minutes or until lightly browned. Transfer to wire racks to cool.

Quick and Easy Sugar Cookies

Makes about 4 dozen cookies.

1 cup granulated sugar

1 cup butter or margarine, softened

1 teaspoon vanilla extract

⅛ teaspoon nutmeg

1 egg

2 ⅓ cups all-purpose flour

½ teaspoon baking soda

Colored decorator sugar

Preheat oven to 375°F. Cream together granulated sugar and butter until light and fluffy. Stir in vanilla extract, nutmeg, and egg. Stir in flour and baking soda. Shape dough into 1-inch balls. Arrange balls about 2 inches apart on ungreased baking sheets. Flatten balls using the bottom of a glass that has been dipped in decorator sugar. Bake for 9 to 11 minutes or until set. Transfer to wire racks to cool.

Shortbread Raspberry Kisses

Makes about 3 ½ dozen cookies.

1 cup butter or margarine, softened

⅔ cup granulated sugar

½ teaspoon vanilla extract

2 cups all-purpose flour

½ cup raspberry jam

1 package (12 ounces) foil-wrapped milk chocolate
candies, unwrapped

Glaze:

1 cup powdered sugar

1 tablespoon butter or margarine, softened

1-2 tablespoons milk

Preheat oven to 350°F. In a large bowl, cream together 1 cup butter, granulated sugar, and vanilla extract. Gradually beat in flour. Refrigerate, covered, for 1 hour. Shape dough into 1-inch balls. Arrange balls about 2 inches apart on ungreased baking sheets. Using your thumb, make a ½-inch indentation centered in the top of each cookie. This will cause the dough to crack around the edges. Fill each indentation with ¼ teaspoonful of jam. Bake for 14 to 16 minutes or until edges are lightly browned. Remove from oven and immediately press 1 piece of candy into the center of each cookie. Allow cookies to cool for 2 minutes on baking sheets, then transfer to wire racks to cool completely. Meanwhile, add powdered sugar, 1 tablespoon butter, and milk to a small bowl. Whisk until smooth. Drizzle cookies with glaze.

Star-Studded Ginger Cookies

Makes about 4 dozen cookies.

1 cup firmly packed brown sugar

¾ cup shortening

¼ cup molasses

1 egg

2 ¾ cups all-purpose flour

1 teaspoon baking soda

1 teaspoon ginger

1 teaspoon cinnamon

¼ teaspoon cloves

¼ cup granulated sugar

48 chocolate star candies

Preheat oven to 375°F. In a large bowl, with an electric mixer at medium speed, cream together brown sugar, shortening, and molasses. Beat in egg. Beat in flour, baking soda, ginger, cinnamon, and cloves. Mix until well blended. Shape dough into 1-inch balls. Pour granulated sugar into a shallow bowl. Roll balls in granulated sugar until coated, then place on ungreased baking sheets. Bake for 7 to 9 minutes or until tops are cracked and edges are set. Remove from oven and immediately press 1 piece of candy into the center of each cookie. Allow cookies to cool for 2 minutes on baking sheets, then transfer to wire racks to cool completely.

Sugary Buttermint Cookies

Makes about 4 dozen cookies.

1 cup soft pastel buttermints

½ cup granulated sugar

½ cup butter or margarine, softened

1 egg

1 teaspoon vanilla extract

1 ½ cups all-purpose flour

1 teaspoon baking powder

¼ teaspoon salt

Colored decorator sugar

Preheat oven to 350°F. Seal buttermints and granulated sugar in a plastic food bag or place between two sheets of waxed paper and crush with a rolling pin. In a large bowl, cream together mint mixture and butter. Add egg and vanilla extract. With an electric mixer at medium speed, beat until well mixed. Add flour, baking powder, and salt. With electric mixer at low speed, continue beating until well mixed. Shape dough into 1-inch balls. Roll balls in decorator sugar. Place on ungreased baking sheets. Bake for 10 to 12 minutes or until lightly browned at edges. Transfer to wire racks to cool.

Sweet Cherry Wrap-Arounds

Makes about 4 dozen cookies.

1 cup butter, no substitutions

½ cup granulated sugar

1 teaspoon almond extract

2 ¼ cups all-purpose flour

48 maraschino cherries

Preheat oven to 350°F. In a large bowl, cream together butter and granulated sugar. Stir in almond extract and flour until well blended. Shape a rounded teaspoonful of dough around most of maraschino cherry, leaving an area of the cherry exposed on top of each cookie. Place on ungreased baking sheets. Bake for 10 to 12 minutes. Do not brown. Transfer to wire racks to cool.

White Chip Cherry Snickerdoodles

Makes about 4 dozen cookies.

    2 ½ cups all-purpose flour

      1 teaspoon cream of tartar

      ½ teaspoon baking soda

      ¼ teaspoon salt

      ¾ cup butter or margarine, softened

    1 ½ cups plus 3 tablespoons granulated sugar, divided

      1 teaspoon vanilla extract

      2 eggs

      1 cup dried cherries, coarsely chopped

      1 package (12 ounces) white chips, divided

    1 ½ teaspoons cinnamon

Preheat oven to 350°F. In a medium bowl, stir together flour, cream of tartar, baking soda, and salt. In a large bowl, cream together butter, 1 ½ cups granulated sugar, and vanilla extract. Add eggs, one at a time, beating well after each addition. Gradually beat in the flour mixture. Stir in cherries and 1 ¼ cups white chips. In a small bowl, stir together the remaining granulated sugar and cinnamon. Shape dough into 1 ¼-inch balls. Roll balls in cinnamon-sugar mixture until coated, then place on ungreased baking sheets. Top balls with remaining white chips. Bake for 12 to 14 minutes or just until centers are set. Allow cookies to cool for 2 minutes on baking sheets, then transfer to wire racks to cool completely.

3791206

Made in the USA
Lexington, KY
23 November 2009